LIFEWATCH

The Mystery of Nature

Calf to Dolphin

Oliver S. Owen

Published by Abdo & Daughters, 4940 Viking Drive, Suite 622, Edina, Minnesota 55435.

Library bound edition distributed by Rockbottom Books, Pentagon Tower, P.O. Box 36036, Minneapolis, Minnesota 55435.

Printed in the United States.

Cover Photo credit: Peter Arnold
Interior Photo credits: Natural Selection, pages 11-12
                       Peter Arnold, pages 7, 10, 25, 28
                       Stock Market, pages 5, 9, 17, 18, 22, 25, 27
                       Animals Animals, pages 14, 15, 21

Edited By: Bob Italia

LIBRARY OF CONGRESS CATALOGING-IN-PUBLICATION DATA

Owen, Oliver S., 1920-
       Calf to Dolphin / Oliver S. Owen.
           p.   cm. -- (Lifewatch)
       Includes bibliography references and index.
       ISBN 1-56239-292-1
       1. Dolphins -- Juvenile literature. 2. Porpoises -- Juvenile
literature.   [1. Dolphins. 2. Porpoises.]   I. Title.
II. Series: Owen, Oliver S., 1920-   Lifewatch.
QL737.C432094   1994
599.5'3--dc20   94-19967
                                                  CIP
                                                  AC

Contents

The Dolphin

Have you seen a porpoise or dolphin leap from the water and dive through a hoop? Have you seen it leap ten feet into the air to grab a fish from the hand of its trainer? Perhaps you have—either on TV or in person at Marineland in Florida. Certainly such "tricks" have made dolphins the most popular animals of the sea. Dolphins and porpoises look alike. However, you can easily tell them apart. The snout of the dolphin ends in a narrow beak. The porpoise has no beak. Porpoises and dolphins are very similar in their behavior. From here on we shall lump these animals together and call them dolphins.

Dolphins belong to a large group of animals called mammals. All mammals, whether dolphins or humans, are fed with their mother's milk. Mammals give birth to their young. In fishes, the female lays eggs in the water. The young fish then hatch from these eggs. Mammals are warm-blooded—the temperature of their bodies remains the same, even though the temperature of the air, land, or water changes. Fish are cold-blooded—their body temperature changes with that of the water in which they live. Dolphins and all other mammals breathe air with lungs. Fish breathe with gills.

Dolphins can be trained to perform tricks like jumping through hoops.

Dolphins breathe air through a nostril, or blowhole, at the top of the head. They come up for air about once a minute. When they exhale they often make a loud puffing sound. Some people call them "puffing pigs." If dolphins did not come up for air, they would drown. Like all mammals, dolphins have hair. Once I found a dolphin stranded on an Oregon beach. I looked all over for some hair and finally found a few bristles on its snout!

Dolphins may look like fish, but they are not closely related at all. They are actually very small whales. They are closely related to the blue whale—the biggest animal this world has ever seen. The dolphins only get to be about eight feet long. The blue whale, however, grows to a length of 220 feet—about the length of a jumbo jet! That's about 27 times that of a dolphin! Like all whales, dolphins swim with a broad, flat tail, or fluke, which moves up and down. (The tail of a fish moves from side to side.) All dolphins have a pair of paddle-like front limbs called flippers. They aid in steering the animal. Hind legs are missing.

You can see the flippers on this dolphin. They help steer the animal.

Notice the blowhole with air bubbles coming out on top of this dolphin's head.

Intelligent Behavior

Scientists consider the chimpanzee to be the most intelligent animal after humans. However, dolphins are not too far behind. In fact, they are thought to be smarter than dogs. We could guess that dolphins are bright simply by looking at their brains. In fact, the dolphin brain looks a lot like yours and mine. It has a lot of wrinkles!

The intelligence of dolphins is shown by the tricks thousands of them have learned in amusement parks, aquaria and zoos throughout the world. Some of them can learn to jump through flaming hoops. Some have been trained to "walk" backwards on the water with their muscular tail fluke, or "throw" balls through nets. Still others have learned to leap out of the water to a height of 20 feet and then ring a bell with their snout or seize a fish held by their trainer. Some dolphins have learned to leap out of the water in a group formation.

Scientists believe that the ability to learn simply by watching a human is a sure sign of high intelligence. If that is true, then dolphins should be considered very bright. For example, a dolphin named Mitzie learned to lift the latch on the gate which closed off her pen, push open the gate, and escape into a larger pool. And she was able to do this simply by watching her trainer do it just a few times!

This dolphin performs at an aqua marine park.
It has learned to jump high into the air.

Animals that help each other out, or cooperate, are also considered intelligent. After all, in order to cooperate with other animals, a certain amount of thinking is needed. Chimpanzees and monkeys are capable of cooperation. But so are dolphins! They travel in "families" and help each other find food or escape from an enemy.

A "family" often consists of about 12 individuals. There is usually an older male that serves as a "leader." Also included are several females with their babies and a number of immature males and females. Sometimes one adult female will look after the young while the other females search for fish. Dolphins have even been known to lift up the head of an injured family member so it wouldn't drown!

Dolphins travel in "families" and assist each other in finding food.

Echo-location or Sonar

Dolphins are able to locate underwater objects by a remarkable system called echo-location or sonar. Bats also use such a system. However, the dolphin's system is

These mysterious creatures have a communications system that resembles radar.

much better. Scientists are not sure which organ makes the sound. It may be made in the throat or in the windpipe. The sound passes through the top of the head. It then leaves the body through the blowhole. If an enemy like a big shark is swimming directly ahead of a dolphin about 100 yards away, the dolphin cannot see the shark because the water is too cloudy.

However, the dolphin doesn't have to see this enemy to know that it is there. The dolphin beams sounds directly in front of it through its blowhole. The sounds travel rapidly through the water. Scientists describe these sounds as short clicks, whistles or squeaks. They are made at the rate of one to 500 per second. The greater the distance of the target, the lower the rate of clicks. If these sounds "hit" the shark, they will then bounce off its body as an "echo."

These echoes give the dolphin a lot of information. They tell the dolphin that the object in its path is a shark, give it some idea of its size, direction and shape, and even tell the dolphin how close it is. The dolphin might decide to swim off in another direction. After all, big sharks like to have dolphin for dinner!

The dolphin's sonar system warns the animal if danger is near.

With the help of its sonar system, a dolphin cannot only "see" enemies, but also can find food fishes, as well as rocks or boats in its path. In fact, a dolphin could find its way through its watery world very well even if its eyes were tightly shut. Kenneth Morris, a biologist, proved this with a simple experiment. He "blindfolded" a dolphin by placing rubber suction cups over its eyes. Then he taught the dolphin to choose one of two steel balls that he placed in the water about five feet away. One ball was two and one-half inches in diameter. The other was two and one-quarter inches in diameter. A human would have a tough time telling these balls apart with eyes wide open. But the dolphin could tell them apart "blindfolded"! The dolphin did it with the help of its sonar system.

Swimming Behavior

Dolphins are the swimming champions of the sea. No fish or shark can match their speed—up to 25 miles per hour. Nor can they match the dolphins' ability to thread their way through barriers in their path. The dolphin's speed is made possible because of its very smooth skin, stream-

The dolphin has smooth skin and powerful muscles which allows it to swim with great speed.

lined shape and powerful muscles. Some dolphins can dive to a depth of 1,000 feet. A few years ago Elgin Ciampi, a dolphin expert, was working in the water near the shore with his pet dolphin. He was amazed how the animal darted, at top speed, back and forth between the dock pilings.

These dolphins are swimming in front of a boat at about 20 miles an hour.

The dolphin, of course, was guided by its sonar system. Suddenly, the dolphin swam directly toward Ciampi. Luckily, the dolphin swerved at the last second. Otherwise it would have rammed right into him. The collision would have killed Ciampi instantly.

Dolphins often like to swim just ahead of boats. They ride the wave pushed up by the prow. Sometimes they swim behind a boat, somewhat playfully, and follow it for miles. From time to time, they will leap high out of the water and even turn somersaults.

Dolphins must come to the surface every minute to get a breath of air. They do this by making a wheel-like "roll." The sight of a hundred dolphins "rolling" all at the same time is one of the ocean's most exciting shows.

Feeding Behavior

Very seldom does a dolphin travel on an empty stomach. There simply is no reason for it. After all, they can outswim and catch

You can see the many teeth on this dolphin.

any fish they would like to eat. Dolphins have plenty of teeth, over 100 in some species. However, they use these teeth only to grasp fish. Dolphins do not chew their food. They simply swallow fish whole. Feeding dolphins often travel in schools, in groups of about 12 to 200 individuals. Members of such schools often cooperate in finding and catching fish. For example, a few dolphins might "nose around" in the ocean bottom. This may flush out fish like sea bass and grunts from their hiding places among the rocks.

As these fish come into view they are easily snapped up by other dolphins waiting nearby. Several dolphins will often work together in herding marsh minnows toward the shore. Once "cornered," the minnows are quickly eaten.

Some open water fish, like sea catfish, travel in huge schools, shaped something like a ball. Dolphins will quickly surround such a catfish school. They will then gobble up any catfish that tries to

Dolphins cooperate with one another when hunting for food.

escape. Some of the dolphins will swim directly into the center of the school and stuff themselves with the tasty fish. Such cooperative behavior may continue for almost an hour. By that time most of the dolphins will have been well fed! The sea catfish is a favorite dolphin food item.

However, they have sharp spines just behind their head. These spines could slice up the dolphin's throat. So the dolphin seizes the catfish tail first. Then it breaks off its head by biting it, shaking it, or rubbing it against sharp rocks. It is a strange sight to see hundreds of catfish heads bobbing on the waves.

Dolphins will often follow shrimp boats off the Florida coast. The fishers drag a net along the ocean bottom to catch the shrimp. Such activity flushes out large numbers of fish. They quickly wind up in the stomachs of waiting dolphins. Commercial fishers often accuse dolphins of "stealing" valuable food fishes which they themselves are trying to net. Such complaints are not based on fact.

A few years ago some scientists made a study of the dolphin's food habits. They opened up the stomachs of dead dolphins that had floated to shore. Their findings took the dolphins "off the hook." True, the dolphins eat shrimp, but dolphins eat mainly less valuable fish like croakers, drum, sardines, and eels which are not sought by commercial fishers.

The Causes of Dolphin Death

Dolphin populations have dropped off greatly along the coasts of the United States. Thousands of dolphins may be killed by a certain kind of animal too small to be seen without a microscope! When these animals become abundant the ocean turns reddish in color. Some people then call it a "red sea" or "red tide." In 1987 and 1988, hundreds of dead dolphins washed up on shore from Florida to New Jersey. Biologists were both alarmed and puzzled. What could have caused the death of all these dolphins? The scientists took samples of the ocean. After many months of hard work, they found the cause of the dolphin die-off—a deadly poison given off by the microscopic "red sea" animals. The dolphins got the poison after eating contaminated fish. During the die-off, scientists counted 20 million of these tiny animals in just one quart of ocean water. Almost half of the dolphin population off the Atlantic coast was destroyed. Dolphins do not have many young. So it may be 100 years before their numbers return to normal.

Thousands of dolphins are killed each year worldwide because they get stranded on beaches. It is hard to explain why this happens to an animal that is such an excellent swimmer. Some scientists believe that dolphins get stranded when their sonar stops working properly. The dolphin I found stranded on an Oregon beach did not look sick. It didn't look injured. There were no tooth marks on it. Maybe its sonar wasn't working any more. So it did not "see" the sand bar into which it was heading.

Many dolphins live in shallow water near the coasts of sub-Arctic oceans. In summer, there is plenty of open water in which to swim about. However, in winter, shelves of ice form and close off small pockets of water. Dolphins may get trapped in such icy "prisons." Large numbers have been killed in this way.

Scientists are baffled by what causes dolphins to get stranded and die.

Very few ocean creatures can match the 25 mile per hour speed of a dolphin. Not too many ever succeed in having a dolphin for "dinner." However, there are a few exceptions. One dolphin-killer is the great white shark. Some of these sharks grow to a length of 25 feet—three or four times the length of most dolphins.

This dolphin is being saved by these scientists after it was caught in a fisher's net.

Scientists do not know too much about shark attacks on dolphins. However, at least in the Bay of Fundy, northeast of Maine, it happens quite frequently. A dolphin will often escape from the shark even after attacked, evident from the tooth marks that the sharks leave on dolphins.

The killer whale, which gets to be 30 feet long, also feeds on dolphins. This does not happen too often because the dolphin and killer whale usually live in different parts of the ocean. Beach strandings, ice-trapping, and enemies like sharks and killer whales cause the deaths of thousands of dolphins each year. But humans are the greatest dolphin-killers of them all. This is really surprising. After all, the dolphin's playfulness and ability to learn tricks have delighted people of all ages. Furthermore, dolphins have become very popular as acrobatic "stars" in the movies and on television. But, despite this popularity, humans have destroyed large numbers of them in the past few decades. The natives of many northern countries, including China and Japan, hunt them vigorously. They eat their tasty meat and use their oil for lubrication.

Millions of dolphins have drowned after getting tangled up in nets put out by fishers. They also die in salmon and cod nets off of Newfoundland, Canada. Tuna fishers cause the greatest number of deaths. Dolphins are found together with tuna in the eastern Pacific Ocean. They often swim just above the schools of tuna. Scientists do not know why. However, the tuna fishers make use of this curious behavior. If they spot a school of tuna, they will lower their nets in that area. But they will kill many dolphins. Tuna fishers killed hundreds of thousands every year during the 1960s and early 1970s. To stop this killing, Congress passed the Marine Mammal Protection Act in 1972. Tuna fishers were required to have federal inspectors on their boats. They could not kill more than 20,000 dolphins a year.

In 1990, several large tuna canning companies refused to buy tuna from any fishers that accidentally killed dolphins. Such protection should put an end to this most frequent cause of dolphin death.

Breeding Activity

Dolphins become sexually mature at three to seven years, depending on the species. The male and female have a playful courtship. Sometimes they will rush at each other and collide with a loud noise. Sometimes one will jump high in the air and come down with a big splash. The pair will often stroke each other with their flippers. They may rub their snouts together. They twist and turn and cause the water to gurgle, bubble and foam. During all this courtship play, they make a constant chatter of whistles and clicks. Such courtship is followed by mating. The male introduces sperm into the body of the female. The sperm unite with eggs made by the female's ovary. This is called fertilization (fer-till-uh-ZAY-shun). The fertilized egg is known as an embryo (EM-bree-oh). It begins to grow inside a muscular chamber called a uterus (YU-tur-us).

After one year the embryo develops into a baby dolphin. Then the mother is ready to give birth. You were born headfirst. However, the baby dolphin is born tailfirst. If its head were in the water too long, it would drown.

Dolphins have a playful courtship, often stroking each other with their flippers.

During the courtship, dolphins chatter with each other using whistles and clicks.

The normal birth of the dolphin takes about 20 minutes. If the mother dolphin has a tough time giving birth, the midwife will then "pull" on the baby to help it out of the mother's body. The newborn baby, called a calf, weighs about 25 pounds—about three times as much as you weighed when you were born. A calf is rarely born dead. The mother may hold her dead calf with her flipper and swim with it.

A newborn calf must breathe just a few seconds after its birth. Otherwise it will drown. The mother and midwife push the baby up to the surface of the water. The calf then takes its first breath. Afterward, it dives down to the mother and starts feeding. As soon as the calf places its mouth on her milk gland, the mother quickly squirts some milk into it. Milk-drinking must not take too long. About twice each minute, the calf has to swim to the surface to get more air. The calf continues to nurse for about 16 months. During this time, it is carefully protected by the mother and midwife.

The male dolphins often swim ahead of the calf and her mother. They look out for any shark that might try to have the calf for "lunch." When danger threatens, the baby dolphin will dart under its mother's body for protection. If the calf does something wrong, it may be disciplined. The mother will give it a gentle bite or may bump it with her snout.

When the young dolphin is about one year old, it will stop nursing and start eating fish. It will grow rapidly. In a few years, it will be a full-grown adult. Some dolphins, such as the acrobatic "stars" of movies and TV, will weigh more than 400 pounds and may get to be 15 feet long.

The mother dolphin feeds and protects her calf up to 16 months.

We have followed the breeding activity of the dolphin from the courtship of the adult, to the mating act, to fertilization of the egg, to development of the embryo, to birth of the calf, and back to the adult once again. It's an amazing story, don't you think?

A mother dolphin and her calf.

Glossary

Blowhole   the opening at the top of the dolphin's head through which it breathes.

Calf   the baby dolphin.

Echo-location   location of objects by "bouncing" sound waves off of them.

Fertilization   union of a sperm with an egg.

Flippers   the flattened front limbs of a dolphin.

Mammal   a group of animals which have hair and in which the mother nourishes her young with milk.

Marine Mammal Protection Act   an act passed by Congress to protect dolphins, porpoises and whales.

Midwife   a female dolphin who helps the mother during the birth of the calf.

Nursing   the act in which the mother dolphin feeds the calf with milk from her milk glands.

Red sea   a part of the ocean which has turned red because of the presence of large numbers of microscopic animals.

School   a large number of fish or dolphins that travel close together.

Sonar   a system for locating objects by "bouncing" sound waves off of them.

Index

Bibliography

Burton, Robert. *The Life and Death of Whales.* New York: Universe Books, 1980.

Caldwell, David K. and Melba C. Caldwell. *The World of the Bottle-nosed Dolphin.* New York: J. B. Lippincott Co., 1972.

Ciampi, Elgin. *Those Other People: The Porpoises.* New York: Grosset and Dunlap, Inc., 1972.

International Union for Conservation of Natural Resources. *Dolphins, Porpoises and Whales of the World.* Washington, D.C., Island Press, 1991.

About the Author

Oliver S. Owen is a Professor Emeritus for the University of Wisconsin at Eau Claire. He is the coauthor of *Natural Resource Conservation: An Ecological Approach* (Macmillan, 1991). Dr. Owen has also authored *Eco-Solutions* and *Intro to Your Environment* (Abdo & Daughters, 1993). Dr. Owen has a Ph.D. in zoology from Cornell University.

To my grandson, Amati,
may you grow up to always
appreciate and love nature.
— Grandpa Ollie